MW00626409

COMMANDING
Life
365
Daily Inspiration

Commanding Life 365 Daily Inspiration

Copyright © 2018 by Commanding Life

For information about permission to reproduce selections from this book, e-mail hello@commandinglife.com

Cover photo by Jordan Wozniak via Unsplash

www.CommandingLife.com

ISBN 978-1-7325400-2-6

GET INSPIRED

Start any time with these daily inspirational messages that help you find focus and feel encouraged. Use them to power the creation of the life you desire. You have 365 new chances to design the day you want.

 DAY 1

For the next year I am committed to becoming who I need to be to live the highest vision for my life. I have all that I need and want as life flows to me and I flow with it. As I work on my purpose, I am Divinely guided, supported, protected and loved. Thank you, Universe, for always steering me toward the best life has to offer me. Amen.

>>>———————————<<<

COMMANDING LIFE

 # DAY 2

Love everything about your life. Trust the process because every circumstance has a higher plan, even if you don't understand the purpose. You may not be where you want to be but take time to see the beauty in your progress. Keep going and trust that your sorrow will be joy, your loneliness will be love, and your lack will be plenty.

 # DAY 3

Do something that makes you laugh, brings joy, and builds your spirit. These moments are essential to your well-being. You spend a lot of time taking care of others, spend a moment taking care of you today. It is important to fill your heart with love and fill your spirit with positive visions for your future. A full spirit is a creative spirit.

 # DAY 4

Remember there is enough happiness for everyone, especially YOU. Life is to be loved and lived; find joy in every moment. Rejoice in your journey, it is what shapes, builds, and molds you into who you need to become. You must go down to understand the joy in being on top. Embrace where you are, accept happiness is yours, and go for it.

You are doing the best you can with what you know; learn to trust yourself more. You have been working hard to create the life you want, now believe it will happen for you. Remember, you are not given a path or purpose without the provisions you need to succeed. Keep moving forward.

 DAY 6

Focus on loving you a little bit more. Do this by giving yourself the time, love, and patience you need because your happiness is key. Be careful what you tell yourself about yourself because you will go out and validate those words. Honor yourself by celebrating your successes and keep doing the best you know. You are enough.

>>>———————————<<<

 DAY 7

Remember that you have created amazing things in your life before and right now is no exception. Stay strong, step up, and embrace your powers of creation. Now is your time to manifest the abundance you want to see in your life. Believe you are supported and have already been given what you need to succeed.

 DAY 8

Before you move forward, take time to celebrate who you are becoming and how you created that change. You have been shedding old habits and working on a new you, therefore stop and observe how amazing taking control of your happiness feels. You are doing a fantastic job. Keep going and don't give up!

DAY 9

It is important to always tell yourself a positive story about yourself. Today remember how incredible you are doing on your journey. See your daily steps and stumbles as learning and progress. Stay positive and believe you can. You have prayed, prepared and worked. It will soon be your time to receive.

# DAY 10

Let today be a day of transformation. Start with changing doubt into DO and making a statement that empowers you to act. Today don't doubt your abilities but DO what needs to be done to create the life you want. Declare "I do have the power to create the happiness I want." Now go out and get it.

 # DAY 11

Connect with the people you are most thankful for today. Make it a habit to regularly express gratitude to them for loving you and helping you on your journey. Thank them for encouraging, inspiring and supporting you. They are part of your story. Celebrate your cheerleaders.

DAY 12

Sometimes life must change so you can change. Embrace these experiences as they are designed to show you how amazing you are. Life is a fantastic teacher. Be an eager and excited student because the faster you learn, the quicker you move on to the next stage. Today get excited about your progress and your passing grades.

# DAY 13

Today take ownership of your dreams and focus on bringing them into reality. Trust that the Universe is working behind the scenes to help make them come true. Trust that what you are working toward will happen. Release your doubt and have faith that what's yours will find its way to you. Life is always working for you.

DAY 14

Change your relationship with others by changing your relationship with yourself. Trusting and loving yourself more will get you unstuck, find happiness, and help with the healing of your heart. Connect with the real you by having faith in your abilities. Develop your strength to overcome what holds you back by believing in you more.

>>> ———————————— <<<

 # DAY 15

Doors are occasionally closed so you can be redirected. Sometimes you are forced to move so you can move forward. Accept the closed door, trust the process, and look hopefully for the new opportunities. A closed door does not mean you are denied; it just means you are delayed.

# DAY 16

Doubt is a powerful emotion
that stops you from feeling you
deserve anything good.
Everyone experiences moments
when they think they won't
ever be happy again. Today
overcome your uncertainty
with faith. Trust the process
and believe you will have all the
success, happiness, and
abundance life has to offer.

# DAY 17

Build a foundation of self-support and encouragement by dismissing doubtful words. Replace them with encouraging words. Rephrase thoughts that don't serve your happiness and regain your control. Uncertainty will always creep in, push it aside and decide only to accept the thoughts that help you achieve your goals.

DAY 18

Today take a moment to find a sense of balance, peace, and strength by taking a minute to refresh and regroup. Use this time to focus on the light on your face and release the darkness behind you. Let go of the weight of your past and open up to the possibilities of the future. Ground yourself with the hope that all will be well by believing and declaring "All is well."

COMMANDING LIFE

# DAY 19

Stop, close your eyes, take a deep breath, and release everything that is not serving your happiness today. As you release it all, let go and stay in the now, don't worry about tomorrow. This moment of stillness is where you reclaim your joy and listen for the answers to keep moving forward. Just pay attention for inspiration.

>>>———————————<<<

# DAY 20

Today remember there isn't just one path to happiness. Everyone's journey is personal and filled with unique twists and turns. You must trust that your plot twist will take you to a beautiful place beyond your experiences and imagination. Sometimes you cannot see the infinite possibilities intended for you. Keep going, my friend.

# DAY 21

You cannot fail in life; you can only find. Trials help you discover who you are, who you are not, and what is truly important to you. Whenever you feel you are failing, ask yourself, "What can I find?" The answer will change your perspective, open you up to possibilities, and set you back on track to your happiness. What can you find today?

>>> ———————————— <<<

# DAY 22

When difficult times appear,
don't become impatient with
outcomes, others, or yourself.
Trust that things are just
delayed and need more time to
work out. Today stay
persistent, focused; keep
trying, and most of all, practice
self-compassion. Keep doing
the best you know with what
you have. Be patient with
yourself.

☀ DAY 23

Each day is a blessing filled with abundant opportunities. Be amazed by what you have conquered and all you have achieved. Acknowledge the beauty in the process of becoming the best you. If you cannot celebrate what you have, celebrate what you have overcome and who you are becoming. It will be an amazing day today.

>>>————————————————⟨⟨⟨

DAY 24

Today push past the feelings of impatience because the need to rush can contribute to your unhappiness. You cannot force life to give you results on your timeline. Stay patient, flow and allow life to unfold before you. Life's joy is in the journey, not the destination. Don't miss the beautiful moments of today being focused on tomorrow.

# DAY 25

There is power in the words you think and tell yourself. Use them to build a strong foundation of confidence that no one can break down. Believe and trust in your abilities by remembering to rejoice in your progress. You are amazing and have accomplished so much. Celebrate your achievements and focus on your gifts. Keep going, my friend.

DAY 26

Find yourself in love with you first and make your choices from this place. Love, happiness, and fulfillment start to flow toward you when you are living life from a foundation of self-love. You must be enough before you are enough for others. Believing you deserve love and happiness is the first step to inviting and creating it.

 **DAY 27**

Let go of the need for approval from others. All it does is weigh you down with false opinions that prevent you from rising to your true potential. Today put yourself in the position of first by not selling yourself short and second to opinions. You have what it takes to live the life you want. Don't allow anyone to let you doubt your destiny.

>>> ———————————— <<<

# DAY 28

Today acknowledge what encourages you to keep going. Your journey continues. See the beauty in it and find the inspiration to enjoy life more. There are many amazing things still left to accomplish. Focus on what feeds your soul so you can take inspired action to keep creating more of it.

DAY 29

Love is an act of will. You willingly decide to give and receive it to others and yourself. You do not have love; you choose to love or not to love. Today make a choice to start loving you just a bit more and welcome the healing it will bring. Self-love is the foundation of understanding and recognizing real love.

# DAY 30

Make a change today by focusing your energy not on fighting the old, but on building the new. Your past is gone and is only given power if you choose to. Focus on making the happiness you want tomorrow by acting today. The seeds of today are blossoming trees of tomorrow. You can always create something amazing and new!

 **DAY 31**

This storm will be over soon, yet you may not remember how you made it through or how you managed to survive. Trust that when you get out, you won't be the same person who walked in the storm. You will be better, stronger, and more focused on creating your happiness. Remember, storms always end.

# DAY 32

When mistakes are made, you might get down on yourself because you feel you've messed up. Today remember that just because you've made a mistake does not mean you are disqualified. Remember, you don't ever fail, you only learn. Keep going; life always gives you chances to do better and be better.

# DAY 33

You are going to overcome and win. Believe and move forward with confidence. Continue to feel, dream, think, and most importantly, do. Consider every breaking point a breakthrough that is one step closer to the happiness you want. Nothing can stop the happiness that is meant for you. Keep focusing on what you want.

>>> ———————————— <<<

DAY 34

The Universe cannot hear you if you don't communicate. Having a hopeful and confident vision of your life is a powerful prayer. Create a plan, state what you want, let it go and allow it to be answered. Keep putting in the work and prepare for it to happen. Trust your dreams will become your reality because life is always working to satisfy your heart.

Sometimes you must hurt to heal, retreat to rise, and lose to win. Life is about learning and growing despite the odds. Trust in your path because the most beautiful things grow from dirt. Beauty takes time to thrive. Stay patient and trust that it will work out at the right time. Nothing stops nature from blossoming in the right season.

# DAY 36

You can accomplish many things in life if you know what you need to be continually happy and motivated. You won't know what brings you fulfillment unless you have a clear purpose for your life. Purpose is the foundation of lasting happiness. Find what ignites your soul, and you will find what will keep you persevering despite the odds.

# DAY 37

Always believe that things are working in your favor. Before you even know it, your paths are being cleared, obstacles are being removed, and your rewards are being prepared. Despite your current challenges, nothing happens before its time. What is for you will find its way to you. Seasons change, and your harvest will arrive soon.

DAY 38

Everyone has a "picture perfect" version of their life that they are competing with. Disappointment and dissatisfaction sets in when you don't live up to it. Find your happiness by letting go of that version and be open to the real vision life has intended for you. Sometimes your vision is limited from your view. Be open to all possibilities.

DAY 39

If you are not happy with your life, take control and write a new story. Never regret living and pursuing the life you want. Don't settle until you find your happiness and are fulfilled daily. You will grow and evolve. It is ok to redefine your happiness occasionally. It's called a plot twist. Every story needs a few to keep it going.

DAY 40

Nothing remains the same for long, therefore, you need to keep allowing and going with the flow. Be receptive to letting go of the old and embracing the new. Don't fear change, simply embrace and have faith in the possibilities it brings. Let life push you to discover something better and more significant than you could ever imagine.

# DAY 41

Remember, you don't need permission from people that don't see your worth. Stop keeping yourself small because of the opinion of others and their lack of faith in your journey. Today go big, embrace your greatness, and go after the life you want. Your destiny is not tied to others' opinion of your success. You've got this.

>>>———————————————<<<

Sometimes in life you must take a specific journey to get better equipped for your true destiny. Remember, the timing of success is up to God. Trust that if your progress is delayed, paths are being cleared and prepared. Your success will happen at the right time and circumstances. Nothing can deny your destiny.

 **DAY 43**

Push fear to the back and
elevate your faith to the front.
Both require you to believe in
outcomes you cannot see.
Today choose faith and get
focused on your dreams.
Believe what is yours will find
its way to you. The possibilities
and paths with faith are
boundless. Get excited about
the journey.

DAY 44

Today is the perfect day to believe in your purpose, path, and what's promised for you. It is also a great day to believe in the abundant possibilities of where life can take you. Trust that your plan is supported and your path is being cleared ahead of you. Whatever unfolds, have faith and believe nothing is going wrong because your path is part of a bigger plan.

☀DAY 45

Today stop asking the Universe "how," "why," and "when," your victory will happen and open yourself to the blessings in this moment. Let go of control and BE the change you want. Stay present and just BE—BEcome BEcause you BElieve. Rather than question your circumstances, just BE the happiness, peace and prosperity you seek.

>>> ———————————————— <<<

# DAY 46

Trust and allow things to unfold naturally. You don't always end up where you thought you would be, but you still end up where you need to be. Practice gratitude and awareness in this moment by embracing and enjoying the process and your progress. You have come a long way; keep believing, creating and keep going.

☀DAY 47

You are more ready than you think; step up and step out to get the life you want. You have the power to change your thoughts, your response, and your actions to create all you want. Don't wait for life to happen to you, make it happen for you. You have what it takes. Take back your control, be proactive and keep pushing forward.

# DAY 48

Quiet time can be your source of hope and deliverance in a trying time, so don't shy away from it. Today take a second to calm your mind so you can listen. Your heart needs to speak with you to help you decide the direction you need to go. Your soul knows what it needs to heal, to move forward, and to thrive. Get still and listen.

>>> ———————— <<<

☀️DAY 49

Let go of the fears and concerns that hold you back from healing and creating. You can only build the life you want if you have faith and trust that all experiences are for your good. Only question your trials to keep learning and growing from them. Trust that they are preparing you to move forward better equipped for your purpose.

>>> ———————————— <<<

Your past does not define you; it strengthens you. Your unique experiences have given you the tools you need to create the life you want today. Every experience has prepared you for this moment and this test. Draw on those skills and move forward with confidence. Your impossible will become your possible and your path your purpose.

DAY 51

Some days are going to be more energetic than others and some are going to be a breeze, so flow with ease. Just because you aren't where you want to be is not a good reason to give up hope. Don't get stuck on the bad days but consider them learning days. It is up to you to push through and consider every day a good day.

Don't cloud what you want with worry about how and when your victory will happen. Just put it out there and keep navigating toward it with your actions. Stop worrying about how the future will unfold and focus on acting now. Things don't always happen when you want them, but they will. Trust all things are working in your favor.

>>> ———————— <<<

COMMANDING LIFE

# DAY 53

Your past did happen, and now it is gone. Embrace the trials and set yourself free so you can move forward. Give up the fantasy that your life would have been different and stop allowing what others did in the past to affect how you live today. Move forward and leave the past where it is behind you. You can only create change in your now.

DAY 54

Slow down, show up, and tune in for your guidance. The Universe is already communicating what you should do to get where you need to go. Stop and pay attention to the answers for deliverance. In the middle of your difficulties, you must listen for your opportunities. The answers are always around you. Get still and listen.

DAY 55

Today let your prayer be "Thank you for deliverance" not "Please deliver me." If you pray with gratitude for a positive outcome, it means you are due one. Claiming your victory declares that you consider it yours. Today pray with gratitude and don't ask but believe your blessings are already delivered. Keep making room for abundance.

>>> ——————— <<<

 # DAY 56

Arrows can only be shot if they are pulled back. When it feels like life is dragging you back with challenges and difficulties, believe you are being prepared to launch. Stay focused, continue creating, and keep aiming for your dreams. You will hit your target with precision because of your determination to succeed.

DAY 57

Don't get frustrated that it is not happening fast enough, but get focused on making it happen. Don't let doubt distract you from the joy in the journey. Keep doing the best you know with what you have. Your commitment to your success and happiness will pay off soon. Keep trusting, keep preparing and keep working.

>>> ———————— <<<

DAY 58

Don't wait for "someday" or even "Friday" to enjoy your day. See the beauty of being blessed with life every single day. Embrace all that your experiences are offering you with an attitude of gratitude. Count your blessings and prepare for your victory. Today you have a lot to be thankful for, find your strength in that.

DAY 59

Everyone has a specific journey that may be a bit more challenging than others. Don't focus on what's going wrong, stay focused on what's going right. Today set an intention to create more of what is important to you. Believe you have what you need to get the job of happiness and victory in your life done.

 DAY 60

True happiness is about letting go of what you assume your life is supposed to be and appreciate it for what it is. Today be at peace with where you've been and stay grateful for what you have. Your life is good, and you will keep working on making it great. You have what you need to get it done.

☀ DAY 61

Don't lose sight of the horizon. Even though you do not see it, know that it is always there. Create a foundation of gratitude so strong that you see the finish line from your lowest and your highest points. Being grateful for the trying times gives you the strength to keep going and rise to your victorious times.

>>> ——————— <<<

Find your best self today by using gratitude to create your happiness, healing, and balance. Appreciation gives you confidence in your ability to create. When you are at your best, finding strength and pushing forward becomes easier. Remember you have the power of creation in your life, and only you can design the experiences you want.

>>>———————————————————<<<

COMMANDING LIFE

☀ DAY 63

Gratitude and positivity can change your perspective and keep you going. Without them, you can lose your way and your hope. Today be thankful for your trying times as well as your triumphant times. They both have a purpose in your journey and created the resilient person you are today. Ground yourself in gratitude.

DAY 64

Make it a habit to be thankful
and regularly express gratitude
to the ones you love.
Appreciate your life and the
fantastic people around you.
They have supported you and
loved you unconditionally.
Thank them for being a part of
your story. Every story needs a
supporting cast; appreciate
yours always.

☀DAY 65

Rejoice that there is a purpose for you every day. You have been equipped and brought to this moment to fulfill something only you can. Embrace today's meaning and continue to go after the best version of your life. Know without a doubt that every single day you are becoming a better you. Keep pursuing your purpose.

You are always looking for a way out, but do you ever look for a way in? If you are stuck and need to move forward, look within for the answers you seek without. Get silent, get focused, and get clear. Don't allow others to create doubt in your heart. Deep down you already know the answer you seek, listen.

Today say to the Universe, "Thank you for carrying me this far." Know that you have been supported and carried, especially when you had no strength to move forward. Believe the Universe is always working with you, for you, and ahead of you. Rejoice that you are always carried and strengthened when you cannot do it yourself.

>>> ——————— <<<

COMMANDING LIFE

DAY 68

Everyone has feelings of uncertainty from time to time, and you won't feel unsure and unbalanced forever. You will feel strong again, so don't fight your feelings or feel guilty for having them. Accept them and be kind to yourself while you ride the doubt out. Don't shame yourself for having feelings. Love, accept, and be compassionate with you.

☀DAY 69

When doors close, choose to feel gratitude for the experience. Recognize that there are other opportunities available to you now. Stop, look up, and open yourself to the possibilities beyond this moment. A closed door can be a blessing as life directs you to where you are supposed to be. You are destined for great things.

>>>———————————<<<

DAY 70

Your hard work will pay off
because your blessings are on
the way! All you need to do is
get your receiving hands ready.
Rejoice and make room in your
life for all that you work for.
Remember, the first step in
receiving happiness is believing
you deserve it. Keep preparing
and know that joy, peace and
love is finding its way to you.

DAY 71

Today spend a moment focusing on and connecting with what you want to manifest in your life. Let that vision create hope for a positive outcome. Let that moment of hope inspire you to find the way to your "how." You have the power to act and create the change you want in your life. Stay hopeful and faithful that it will work out soon.

# DAY 72

Today when you pray and express gratitude for having what you want, take it a step further and open yourself to listening and receiving guidance to get it. We all have things we want to ask and say to God. But remember, He also has things He wants to tell us. Get still and listen for your guidance. Your prayers will be answered.

# DAY 73

Let it be—three essential words to guide you today. So often, energy is spent overthinking outcomes that never happen. Don't miss out on the beauty of the journey, just let life unfold by allowing your blessings to line up or come around to you again. Trust in divine timing. Nothing is going wrong.

DAY 74

Believe that your experiences are always working for you and ahead of you to prepare you. Trust that paths are being cleared and obstacles will be removed. The divine possibilities don't ever reveal themselves clearly, but know that what is for you will always find its way to you. Your destiny can never be denied.

☀ DAY 75

Trust that the Universe is always on your side. Even when you have twists and turns on your journey, they are designed for your good. Learn to receive the lesson and allow life to rise up and support you. You cannot do it all or be it all. Ask for help when needed and accept support when given.

>>> ———————————— <<<

# DAY 76

Don't shy away from the happiness you want with self-doubt and negative thoughts. Instead of getting stuck in self-resistance, focus on positive persistence. Don't give up on creating what you want, believe it is yours. You have what it takes to create the happiness you desire. It is up to you to go out and get it.

☀DAY 77

Make today about acceptance. Accepting your right now, your path, and your life as is. Take what is being offered and use your gifts to find your way. When you truly embrace the hand you have been dealt, then you can repurpose it and create what you want. You are a powerful creator with the ability to reshape your life and happiness.

>>> ———————————— <<<

# DAY 78

Some of the most successful people at some point doubted their destiny. What made them great is that they never gave up on themselves. Don't let fear freeze you into not moving forward. When you find yourself in doubt, go deep within and remember who you are. Allow your strength to pull you through and onward.

Sometimes when you force things to happen before its time, you are met with obstacles and challenges. Resistance is just a message that you aren't quite there yet. Learn to go with the flow regardless of the timing. Focus on what else needs to be prepared to receive your blessings. Nothing can stop what is meant for you, not even time.

# DAY 80

When you are down, the only way you can go is up. Don't let your current position discourage you, keep going and stay persistent. Know that the only way forward is to keep pushing. Pursue your happiness by believing there is only one way you can go and that is to the finish line. Don't rest, rise.

 DAY 81

There is a difference between being faithful to a plan and "faith full" to God's plan. When you are too faithful to the wrong path, you don't know when to let go and change course. When you are full of faith, you understand that what's for you will always find you no matter where you stand. Stay faith FULL, my friend.

DAY 82

Today ask for support, the ability to overcome, and the courage to see past this moment of time. Ask for the courage to push beyond your doubt. Let your prayer be, "Thank you for all the good in my life and the good on its way into my life. Thank you for the strength to continue believing and knowing all will be well, because all is well. Amen."

 DAY 83

Today focus on your growth, develop your magic, and ground yourself toward a more balanced life. Harmony, abundance, peace, and happiness flow to those who are aligned for it. Receive what you want by being what you want. Position yourself and your heart for abundant possibilities by believing they are yours and they flow easily to you.

>>>———————————————————<<<

DAY 84

Today pray for the patience and faith to keep trusting in yourself and your happiness. Pray for the courage to continue loving, healing, and most of all, pray for the strength to keep going. Pray and prepare your mind to receive the best life has to offer. You must have faith in the fulfillment of your happiness. Believe in your prayers.

>>>———————————<<<

DAY 85

Are you paying attention to what increases your energy and what takes away from it? Your internal guidance system is continuously letting you know what you should move toward and away from. Move in the direction of what ignites your soul and listen for what you need to create more. It may be the key to your happiness, fulfillment and purpose.

>>>———————<<<

DAY 86

Be careful not to act because of struggle, pain or anger, as these emotions take away your power of creation. Today work on being proactive, not reactive based on your circumstances. Happiness is created when you are intentionally working on the life you want. You are in control of your happiness. Only you can captain your ship.

 **DAY 87**

Don't just take action, take inspired and purposeful action. When you act with intent, the magnificent manifests. Give power to every step you take by moving with confidence and trust that all will be well. Keep pushing forward to a better way, even better than you can imagine. Believe every step you take has a divine purpose and will take you closer to happiness.

>>>—————————————<<<

 DAY 88

Finding balance when you are uncertain begins with finding what grounds and empowers you. Only you know what you need to thrive. It may be difficult at times but stay true to your healing and focus on what ignites your soul. The hardest part of healing is accepting that you are not where you want to be. Keep going. You will be fulfilled.

 # DAY 89

Remember, you attract what you put out—intentionally and unintentionally. The more positive the vibe, the more you enjoy your life (and it loves you back). Today get picky about where you go and what you choose to partake in and who you participate with. Today surround yourself with positive people and positive vibes only.

# DAY 90

Today claim success in your life. Live as if you already have the victory. What you dream about and what you work so hard for, trust that it is yours and it will manifest. You must believe you deserve every moment of the triumph that is about to come. Have faith that you've already won by preparing for the celebration. Plan a party.

 **DAY 91**

Today allow yourself to consciously choose your response in trying situations. There are times to act, times to stay still, times to respond and times to let it go. Whatever action you decide to take, do it with a positive intent focused on your peace. Take control of your happiness and your destiny with the power in your response.

>>> ———————— <<<

DAY 92

Today improve your life by learning to control where your attention goes. What you concentrate on will expand, so focus on the positive. Don't get sucked into situations that don't uplift you. Value your time and direct your energy toward creating the life you want. You have been working hard at your happiness, celebrate that.

☀️ DAY 93

Today step back a bit, regroup, and figure out how to step forward. Sometimes you need to stop, recharge, then return wiser and more determined with a solid plan to manifest your dreams. You don't always have to be on the go. Today shift into neutral and see where you need to make your next turn. Look for your guidance.

>>>———————————<<<

# DAY 94

Understand the difference between your wants and your needs. There are many things you want, but it may not be what you need right now. Make sure you have what is essential to your happiness so that you are equipped to work toward what you want. Fill your heart with joy, peace and abundance then work on your reality.

>>>————————————————————————<<<

DAY 95

What you say to yourself may seem insignificant to you, but remember your words can encourage or discourage your actions. Today take control and be more deliberate in what you say. Keep it positive to support the success you are working on. Be your loudest and most positive cheerleader.

DAY 96

Don't lose faith when your story gets tough. Remember, you don't always have a say in when things happen, but you can always decide to stay optimistic while you work and prepare. Regain control by looking for the silver lining through life's twists, turns and lows. There is power in positivity. Stay confident that your blessings are on the way to you.

☀DAY 97

It is time to put your plan into action. What are you waiting for? You have done the work now leap. You have the tools, the talents, and the skills necessary. Now is your time. Don't wait, go for it and win. Believe you are always prepared and have the provisions you need to pursue your path and fulfill your purpose. Nothing blocks purpose.

DAY 98

You are always there for others. Today be there for yourself. Taking an occasional moment is not selfish; it is "self first." Show up for yourself so you are better supported to show up for others. You earned the time from your constant service to others, now spend some on you. Your dreams are important too.

DAY 99

You believe so much of yourself
and who you are on any given
day, but one of the most
important truths you can hold
is that happiness is yours.
Change your day with one
grounding thought: "I know
that happiness is mine and I
have an unlimited supply in my
life." Believing you have it gives
you the strength to create
more of it. Now go for it.

>>> ———————————————— <<<

DAY 100

Going through things you'd never thought you'd go through will only take you places you never thought you'd get to go. Keep pushing through to get to where you are destined to be. Embrace your life and all the fantastic possibilities. Believe things are always working in your favor and know that when you can only see a few, God delivers many. Flow with life as it unfolds.

No matter how tough life gets or how discouraged you feel, continue to get dressed and show up. Even though circumstances aren't ideal, if you don't show up, you will miss your call to get to the front of the line. You must be present to receive your blessings. Today keep showing up, keep doing, and you will keep winning. Showing up expresses your commitment to your happiness.

DAY 102

Today don't dwell on what went wrong. Instead, focus on what is going right and what to do next. Closed doors and missed opportunities will redirect you to where you need to go. Spend your energy moving forward rather than questioning why things are going wrong. Trust that answers will always be revealed with time. Stay focused on creating.

>>>———————————————<<<

 **DAY 103**

Today affirm that you are who you are because of where you have been. Your negatives do not outweigh your positives. Your past missteps and letdowns have empowered you to navigate in your now. You are always learning, growing, evolving, and rising to better. Spend some time today and celebrate your journey.

No matter where you are standing right now, whether it is a mountaintop or a valley, stop, regroup, and give yourself the very best you have at this moment. Don't settle in your setbacks, but believe in your blessings. Have faith you have everything you need to keep moving forward. It does not matter if you crawl, walk, jump, leap or sprint. Just keep moving forward.

In case no one told you today, you are amazing! Never give up, stay positive, and most importantly, keep creating the life you want. You have the power over what you have in your life. Only you know what satisfies your heart. Don't let anyone discourage you from going after your happiness. It is your life, believe in the abundant greatness of it.

>>>———————————<<<

Life is all about balance and flow. You don't always need to be getting stuff done. Today kick back, relax, and appreciate the joy in the journey. Use this moment to get the revitalization you need physically and mentally to keep going. Balancing yourself occasionally is necessary to keep flowing through challenges and triumphs.

☀ DAY 107

You have come a very long way. You have survived what you thought was impossible and you continue to persevere. You have made it through and will continue to keep pushing through. Today concentrate on those successes. You have triumphed over doubt and many challenges. Take a moment to celebrate all the amazing things you manifested in your life.

Stop looking for your happiness in the future as life is happening right now. You will keep missing the beauty of a moment if you keep looking forward or backward. Missed moments will add up to a lifetime of missed experiences of joy. Today don't lose another moment. Find your happiness and strength by staying in the moment. Be here now.

 DAY 109

Love yourself with the same patience and understanding you give others. Remember, you are your first love. The more you love you, the better you are at loving others, and recognizing those that do. Today give yourself love, appreciation and acceptance. You are a gift to yourself and the world, and you have what it takes to live fulfilled.

Keep making great choices. You are doing a great job. You now realize you cannot have the life you want by practicing old habits. You have welcomed new thoughts and created further actions. Keep working on doing better, being better, creating better and living better. Continue to work on the life you want, and life will exceed your expectations.

Your life vision is for you and no one else, therefore, sometimes others don't see or believe in it. Today remember you were given your vision, and you will be given your provision to complete your purpose. What you need to succeed will always come to you. Stay focused, patient, and continue to pursue your happiness. Don't doubt because others don't see.

Positive thoughts are necessary and help you push past obstacles to transform your current situation. To attract better, you must begin with having thoughts that encourage and build you up. Today claim your victory, stay positive, and believe you can and you will win. You deserve every moment of success you will receive. Have faith and trust in timing.

DAY 13

Stop being hard on yourself for not being where you think you should be. Take a moment to reflect and marvel at your life. What caused you heartache has made you wise. What broke you has made you strong. Despite everything, you still created an amazing life. You are a fantastic person. Be thankful for it all.

DAY 114

The more you improve yourself, the better you feel. The better you feel about yourself, the better you feel about your life. Keep learning and growing and use those positive feelings to drive you to create the results you want in your life. You are the creator of your story. Live by those words.

 DAY 115

Today don't ask for deliverance
from trials, pray for relief from
the things in your heart that
hinder you from finding
contentment. Everyone needs
some form of healing. Once you
release the weight of what
holds you down, you can rise
and discover your happiness.
Find your restoration in what
bring you joy. A healed heart is
a whole heart that receives
more.

There is power in the words you whisper to yourself. Today be mindful and use them to reinforce your confidence and build a solid foundation for your success. Believe and trust in your abilities and rejoice in your progress. You are amazing and have accomplished so much. Keep going.

# DAY 117

Make a change today by focusing your energy not on fighting the old, but on building the new. Yes, your past was tough, but you decide if tomorrow will be as well. Continue focusing on creating the future you want by working at your happiness today. You cannot sit around and wish for change; you have to be the change.

# DAY 118

Today claim success in your life. Live as if you already have the victory you work for. What you dream about and what you work hard for, keep the faith that it will manifest. You must believe you deserve every moment of the win that is about to come. You must live like you have already won. Claiming it lets the Universe know you expect it.

>>> ———————— <<<

COMMANDING LIFE

DAY 119

To succeed, sometimes sacrifice and surrender are necessary to your story. Let go of what's not working and open yourself to welcoming the new. Don't look at the surrender as a failure. Instead, look at it as an opportunity to find the best version of yourself. A more joyful and rewarding life is ready for you. Sometimes you must let go and make room to receive.

DAY 120

Change your thinking and you will change your life. What tests you and keeps you stuck can be transformed into something different when you shift your perception of it. What challenges you was sent to change you. Step back, take a new look, and watch the magic begin when you start to view your life differently. A positive view is the best view.

DAY 121

Today affirm that you are who you are because of where you have been. Your struggles should never overshadow your successes. You have taught yourself how to navigate to your now, so remain confident that you can keep going. Stay learning, growing, and winning; celebrate and continue to be grateful for every step of the journey.

DAY 122

No matter where you are standing, in the lows of a valley, or the peaks of a mountain, give yourself the very best you have at this moment. Trust and believe you have everything you need to keep going higher and achieve your happiness. You are equipped for your path because you know that every day has a purpose. You have everything you need to get the life you want.

>>> ————————————— <<<

DAY 123

You are crushing it! Never give up, stay positive and keep pursuing the life you want. You have the power of creation in your story. Forget past chapters; keep building new ones. And, most importantly, leave an unforgettable mark on everyone you meet. Kindness is never forgotten, but it is always rewarded.

DAY 124

Life is about risk and reward. You don't always need to be getting stuff done and keeping yourself busy. Today remember it is ok to occasionally kick back, relax, enjoy, and reflect on your incredible journey. You have been putting in the work; set aside a moment to celebrate and reward your endeavors. The more you celebrate, the more you get to celebrate.

Finding your footing when you are uncertain begins with finding what grounds and empowers you. Only you know what you need to heal, grow, and regain confidence. It may be difficult at times to keep going, but stay true to your healing and what you need to thrive despite your environment. Ground yourself by believing you are blessed.

DAY 126

Your missed steps and missed takes do not define you. They develop you into the person you have become today. Remember, it is not about the way you start in life or the stumbles you took along the way. It is about how you finish. Today focus on the joy in the race and the feeling of triumph when you cross that victory line. Finish strong.

>>>———————————————<<<

Like a phenomenal Phoenix rising from the fire, you too are ready to climb. You are prepared to live your truth faithfully, fearlessly, and masterfully. You have been prepping for this moment for a long time. Today embrace where you are, rise to the occasion, and give it your best. You have what you need to keep soaring to unbelievable heights.

>>>———————————<<<

Be thankful you are blocked from what you think you wanted, and believe you are being blessed with what you never knew you needed. Life is always working for you, ahead of you and with you. You are continuously supported and given what you need to thrive. Stay grateful for it all and continuously live like you are blessed.

☀ DAY 129

Today's prayer, "Thank you for the more in my life. The abundant blessings, opportunities, mindset and opening doors. Please keep blessing me, supporting me, and helping me cross the finish line. I trust where I am, and I trust where I am going is worth it. You see more for me than I can even imagine for myself and I am grateful for that. Thank you for my amazing life. Amen."

>>> ———————————————— <<<

# DAY 130

Today acknowledge what encourages you to keep going. The journey continues, see the beauty in it and find the inspiration that gives you life. Focus on what feeds your soul and take inspired action to keep creating.

Be thankful you are blocked from what you think you want, and believe you are being blessed with what you never knew you needed. Life is always working for you and with you. Stay grateful for it all.

 DAY 132

Change your thinking and change your life. What tests you, can teach you when you shift your perception of it. Challenges are sent to change your life and push you to your next level. Step back, take a new look and watch the magic begin when you start to view your trials differently.

DAY 133

Hurt makes a heart heavy and keeps you from reaching higher. Letting go of the pain is not about forgetting it, but accepting it happened. Today get unstuck and move forward by finding peace with your experiences. Open your life to where you are meant to be. Welcome the miracles a healing heart can bring.

Happiness is a visitor that goes door to door looking for welcome signs. You must make room in your heart to invite it in. If you don't prepare and put the welcome sign out, it will miss your door. Today clear space in your life to invite happiness in by anticipating the knock at your door. Get excited; your door is next.

DAY 135

Before you step out to get your victory, consider how you run your race. Do you believe your race will be smooth sailing or a stormy ride? The world meets us where we meet it. Today rephrase how you see your race and your victory. Claim calm waters, smooth sailing, and winds working in your favor. Believe life is working with you always.

# DAY 136

Today is an amazing day;
yesterday was an amazing day
and tomorrow will be another
amazing day. Claim it. Amen.

☀DAY 137

Believe that nothing is going wrong and what you are experiencing is necessary to shape you into who you need to be. The person that needs to cross the finish line needs to be strong, full of faith and grateful for the victory. What you are 'growing' through is teaching you how to appreciate your victory walk fully.

>>>———————————————<<<

 DAY 138

Be thankful for every closed door and 'no' you have encountered. These experiences created the strength needed to find the 'yes.' The next time you are stopped with 'no,' say thank you for the rejection and look for the clear direction you are destined to go.

DAY 139

To get good things you have to allow good things. You must open up and permit yourself to become the person that receives only great things. You must believe you are worthy before you can receive it. Today declare, "I am a beautiful, blessed being and I deserve good things, always."

When your energy gets off balanced, it has not accepted your circumstances for what they are. The heart and the head experience conflict because one feels, and the other does not believe. To realign yourself, take a second to listen to both for the truth. Peace will come when you accept a situation for what it is, not what you hoped it would be. Sometimes the heart needs time to align with your head.

DAY 141

You have to believe you are worth every bit of happiness you are working for. Don't hesitate, don't be doubtful, don't worry, keep pushing forward. Stay focused, keep working and claim your happiness because you know you are worthy. Don't let anyone make you doubt your destiny. You will win.

Sharing is defined as having something with another. Giving away is defined as providing something to someone you no longer need. Hearts and lives are to be shared with people you love, not given away. Before you give your heart away, consider what it means to share it instead. You have a heart worthy of sharing

☀DAY 143

Say thank you to everything and everyone that has left you. What left you was never meant to stay, and what remains will never leave you. You are not blessed with what you have lost, you are blessed with what you have left. Use what remains to create the life you want and keep going.

DAY 144

Your best life isn't 'when,' it is happening right now in everything you do. Happiness is found in the way you react; decide to act; and how you love yourself and others. Your best life begins with loving yourself unconditionally; believing in your abilities and using that love to create great things. Your best life starts with you.

DAY 145

"Stop. Not yet. Wait, because I have something better for you," is what the Universe is telling you when it sends an obstacle your way. Instead of getting frustrated you are blocked, get still and see the 'better' it is trying to send to you. Don't get stuck on the 'stop' get excited about the possibilities.

Build a faith so strong that you become too confident to be doubtful, too optimistic to be fearful and too determined to be defeated. Know that what is for you will find you and your destiny will never be denied. Twists and turns are temporary and necessary to guide you to your purpose.

☀DAY 147

What will you create today?
Will it be happiness, healing,
joy, love or peace? You are a
powerful creator, remember
that always. Go out there and
create the heck out of the life
you want, and don't apologize
for it. It is your life, not theirs.

>>>————————————<<<

DAY 148

Love the people that see your magic at your lowest and highest points. Don't get distracted trying to convince the people that don't see the real you. Love the ones that love you back, and believe you are worthy of their love.

It is not your responsibility to save someone by loving them into healing. It is up to them to heal their own heart. It is your duty to heal your heart then share it with others. Self-improvement begins with self-love and self- awareness. A healed heart recognizes another healed heart and knows real love when it arrives.

DAY 150

If you understand time and season, you will never doubt the reason for your delay. Blessings are Divinely timed and cannot be late. Today believe paths are being cleared and your miracles are on the way. You cannot rush what's promised.

DAY 151

Today say good riddance to people and actions that do not support your self-worth. Know that you don't need the acceptance of others, only to believe in yourself, your destiny and your success. Stop looking for external validation of your amazing abilities. Blossom whether you are watered by others or not.

You work very hard to win, but do you put any effort into self-healing? Healing will bring you the victory you are looking for. Understand that every experience you have is designed for your improvement. Your blessings will only come to a heart that is ready for it. Get your heart ready.

DAY 153

You cannot be hard on yourself for needing help, we all need someone to lean on occasionally. You don't know everything, and you cannot be everything. Ask for help if you need it. Learn to recognize and accept a helping hand when it is needed.

DAY 154

Keep yourself in balance and control by always setting a positive intention for your day. You must put yourself first so that you can then be the best for others. Being positive does not mean that things will always be OK. It just means that you have faith that it will be OK no matter the circumstances.

☀ DAY 155

Today is a great day to have faith. Faith that what you hope for, despite not being able to see it, will happen. No one says having faith is easy, but it is necessary for happiness. Nothing is easy at the beginning. Keep learning, growing and going forward.

DAY 156

At some point, you have to let go of what you think should happen and live in what is truly happening. No one wants to face reality, especially when it's not what you want. But in accepting what is real, you will find the way to move forward. Use what you have and create the life you want.

DAY 157

When you get close to your victory line, someone or something is always sent to distract you from crossing. Stay focused and don't let it steer you off course. Declare "Nothing will stop my victory, not today!" Keep going.

God knows right where you are, and He knows exactly where you need to be. Even though things aren't going the way you want them to, trust that every circumstance has a purpose. There is always a lesson to be learned, a skill to be developed or someone to meet before you move forward. Trust the process.

Thank you, Universe, for letting me know when to go, when to stop, when to share and when to receive. Keep guiding me on when to listen, when to release and when to hold steadfast in my faith. Keep leading me toward what I need in my life to thrive. Amen.

 **DAY 160**

You might not have a strong vision for your life, but you do have eyes to look forward with hope you will find it. Your life does not always need a clear plan, only awareness that each day has a purpose. Today, with or without a strategy, take your journey one step at a time. The vision will unfold at the right moment.

DAY 161

Today remember that no matter how many mistakes you make or how slow your progress appears, you are still ahead of everyone who is not trying. You have what it takes to keep going and building. You are a powerful creator and all your hard work will pay off soon.

DAY 162

Your life is not unfolding by chance. What you are currently experiencing has taken months to align and prepare. No matter what the day brings, look at it with gratitude. Seeing the blessings in the minute helps to acknowledge the purpose of the moment. Believe nothing is going wrong.

>>> ———————————————— <<<

DAY 163

The sacrifices you are making now will pay off when it's all said and done. Sometimes you must bury yourself for you to grow into someone new and improved. Your tunnel vision is necessary for the fulfillment of your life's vision. Keep focusing on what you need to achieve to get what you want.

Don't get stuck feeling sorry for yourself. Your blessings are just above you. Today rise toward them by using gratitude to pick yourself up. You already have what you need to complete the race. What you feel down about is what will strengthen you and make you grow. Use what you have and power your purpose.

# DAY 165

Let prayer become your habit and welcome miracles as your lifestyle. Don't give up on believing despite what temporarily comes your way. Pray on the good days and the trying days. Prayer and gratitude will make every day a great day because it can ground and strengthen you. Believe your blessings are on the way.

>>>———————<<<

When you are feeling like a failure, remember the marathons you ran, the mountains you climbed and the stormy seas you navigated through. Don't let one chapter of defeat rewrite the ending of your book. You have what it takes to win, remember who you are and keep crushing it.

No matter how strong you believe you are, you are still human. No one said life would be easy or there won't be a struggle to stay focused. We all want to be seen, loved and accepted for who we are. Remain confident in your abilities. Today be kind to yourself and others, we all need compassion.

DAY 168

We all have pain and power within us, and it is your choice which you use to manifest your purpose. Your pain is part of your journey, and it is what makes you who you are. Embrace and use everything you have learned to become a master mind of your power. You are amazing, believe that.

# DAY 169

You are valuable, lovable and incredible. Don't let anyone take that belief from your heart. Everyone has it tough from time to time, but that does not mean happiness is unavailable. Every heart deserves to be loved, and every face deserves a smile. Keep smiling and loving my friend.

You need to know sadness to know happiness and absence to appreciate the value of presence. Life reveals what you don't want so you understand what you need when it comes. It is amazing that when you think it is working against you, it shows you that it was always on your side. Stay strong.

DAY 171

Make today great by focusing on all that is going well. Put your energy into what you can change and let go of what you cannot. Believe you are supported, your obstacles cleared, and your blessings are being delivered. No matter what is going on, believe it will be a great day.

>>> ———————— <<<

Let go of old habits that are not serving your happiness. Try a new way by releasing and elevating to higher. Change is hard in the beginning, but it is necessary. Be kind to yourself as you try, no one has it perfect. Climbs are never easy and require focused positive energy.

# DAY 173

Have patience today my friend. Yes, you want what you are working hard toward to manifest. But, if you stop and reflect, you will realize that it has already become your reality. Happiness is not when everything falls into place; it is recognizing the miracles of them falling into place. See that you are already blessed.

>>>———————————<<<

 # DAY 174

Accept an invite today or extend one. Use this time to celebrate your progress with the ones you love. Celebrating and acknowledging your success allow you to focus on the positive. Life is lived in the moments of joy we stay present in.

DAY 175

You are amazing. You are blessed. That's all you need to remember. Use what you have and make it a great day.

Say thank you to every door you knocked on that did not open. Rejoice that it did not let you in because it was not meant for you. What is meant for you will open and welcome you. A closed door is designed to redirect and help you discover what you are destined for.

DAY 177

Understand the power of your mind and program it for success. Get up, show up, and set the tone for how you want your day to go. Know that you are always in control of your reactions. Don't let the world take that from you. Today be your mastermind.

☀ DAY 178

Let go of the worry and stress that comes with waiting on the right time. Focus on the peace of knowing it will happen, rather than the pace it is happening. Life must go slow at times, so you can prepare for when it starts to go fast. Appreciate the beauty in the pace and give thanks for the peace.

>>>————————————————————‹‹‹

When you start doubting whether your prayers are being answered, the Universe will surprise you with new opportunities and coincidences. Let go of how you think your blessings should arrive and allow yourself to be amazed by life's generosity. Pay attention to the goodness happening now.

Who is your co-captain, is it fear or faith? Many people go through life with one or the other accompanying them on their journey. Some travel with doubt that good will come to them. Others travel with trust that good still comes despite temporary set-backs. The co-captain is chosen by the captain. Decide who you will flow with today.

Release your attachments to the people, places, and things that hold you back from finding the real you. The most important connection you can seek is the one from within. When you discover who you are, the abundant blessings you seek can then find you.

DAY 182

When you understand there is unity in all things, then the illusion of separateness is gone. All circumstances, trials, and triumphs become necessary to one journey - your journey. You fail so that you are forced forward. You are blocked so you can start believing. Whatever you are experiencing right now, have faith that it is part of one big plan.

DAY 183

Who would you like to spend time with today? When you create your long list of to-dos, don't forget to schedule the most important meeting of the day; one with you. Use that time to reenergize, revitalize and equip yourself to effectively deal with others. Life can be draining, you need to always pour from a full cup.

>>> ———————————— <<<

DAY 184

Take a moment to reflect on what you have gone through, not to live in the past, but to learn from it. Make sure you are not repeating old habits trying to get new results. Honor your progress and keep trusting the process. You have worked diligently to improve yourself and your situation. Today be grateful and celebrate that.

Nothing that negatively impacts your heart, or your life, is easy to move past. You have to keep trying to push through the stages of disappointment, to get to your peace. Change is always hard in the beginning, a big mess in the middle, but beautifully worth it in the end. Don't give up. Focus on the freedom the healing will bring.

DAY 186

Today maybe you woke up with heartache or stressed about things not going your way. Did you focus on that lack or did you focus on your blessings? The Universe is constantly trying to pour healing and abundance into your life. Don't let the lack distract you. Stop asking and start thanking.

# DAY 187

Your life will change for the better when you recognize how gifted you are. No one sees the world like you, love and accept that. You may not be where you want to be, see that is a blessing. You can't rush your success. Sometimes you have to learn the lesson of patience, so you can reap the reward of abundance.

DAY 188

Stop, sit back and truly see the miracles unfolding in your life. Change can be big, or it can be small, either way recognize it is progress. If you don't stop to smell the roses, you won't appreciate the garden you are walking through. Today is a celebration kind of day. Life is good.

 DAY 189

You have the power to create the life your heart wants. Your life on the outside reflects how you live and feel on the inside. How you describe your life to yourself is the way it will manifest. Keep your heart and your whispers positive and abundant goodness will flow easily to you.

>>>———————<<<
COMMANDING LIFE

# DAY 190

Today let your prayer focus on alignment. Alignment of what makes your soul happy, your heart whole, and life worth living. Today pray that distractions are removed, and doors open to welcome good things. Flow to peace, prosperity, and purpose. Let your prayer be "I invite Divine alignment into my life and I am thriving."

DAY 191

Many ignore moments of happiness because they focus on when: "When they have" and "When they do." Happiness exists in those unnoticed moments of miracles happening right now. Today decide to stay present in your experiences and receive the blessings they continuously offer. Being present is a present.

Get familiar with the positive feelings that enable you to thrive. Use that awareness to consciously fill your 'life cup.' Fueling up is necessary for staying grounded when experiences throw you off balance. Life continuously gives, takes, pushes, pulls, and that can be draining if you don't fill up. Learn the art of pouring into your reserves and drawing from them as necessary.

DAY 193

People get trapped living the life they think they should because they are taught conformity and comparison. Free yourself from trying to live like others. You will never get where you need to go walking someone else's path. Listen to what you are called to do, rather than what you think you should do. Align and allow your unique path to unfold and you will thrive.

>>> ———————— <<<

The Universe moves in your favor based on what you do to move your life forward. What you reap is based on your actions, relationship with self, and the attention you place on your emotional health. Consider your heart the seed to your life because what you hold in it will be what grows. Yes, miracles manifest from dirt, but the seed must be healthy enough to thrive.

# DAY 195

Success is not gained from suffering; it is obtained from getting the most out of your life. Everyone struggles, but it is what you create from it that becomes your most significant victory. Today instead of allowing the world to take your strength, fight back by creating a plan for your life. Decide that no matter what comes your way, you will push past it to your victory.

COMMANDING LIFE

DAY 196

Make today about holding firm in your faith. Faith does not mean you will have it easy; it is knowing you will eventually succeed despite struggles. No one is exempt from trying times, but you must keep putting up a good fight. Keep believing in what you work hard for. Faith keeps you climbing when you cannot see the top.

Lifelong love cannot be sustained without forgiveness. Forgive yourself and forgive the ones who have hurt you in the past. Today let go of the hurt that lingers with unforgiveness. Healed wounds help you become whole. It is hard to be at peace if you remain bitter. Move on to better.

Acknowledge what needs improvement, so you can move forward. Not everyone is good at everything, and that is OK. Acceptance of flaws is the best way to pursue the creation of an abundant future. Without the need to be better, you would remain stagnant. Yes, your life is imperfect, but that is what pushes you to grow, try harder and live better.

Make a change in what you pray for. Instead of praying for abundance, peace, and strength, pray for the skills to overcome. Pray for the ability to move beyond what keeps you from finding your plenty. Pray for the release from what someone else did so you can find your clarity. Pray for the healing that opens you up to real love.

DAY 200

Today choose to be three things: teachable, faithful and available. Be teachable and learn what is needed to move forward to create the life you want. Be faithful and believe that good things will always come your way despite setbacks. And lastly, be available to the miracles destined for you. You must show up to get blessed in life.

DAY 201

Everyone has a chapter they don't speak about. Anxiety wins when you shut up, and peace wins when you speak. Suffering is always done in silence. Today pray and speak your hurt so God can answer with your healing. You cannot fix what you don't face. You have the power to write the next chapters.

Be patient and focus on peace, not the pace. If you truly believe something will be yours, it will be. Delays are tests to see how badly you want what you work for. Time pushes you to be creative in your pursuit of what your heart desires. Despite the timing, keep going after what you want. Stay faith FULL, my friend.

Ignored pain never goes away. Your heart wants you to heal, do better and be better. Every struggle you are experiencing is pushing you toward healing. Take it one day at a time, take it one challenge at a time and before you know it your heart will become whole. Life never tests you on the outside it tests you on the inside.

 **DAY 204**

Self-compassion is essential because if you aren't strong enough on the inside, life will break you down on the outside. Learning to love yourself is the foundation that grounds you to be OK no matter what happens. Self-love allows you to remain whole whether what you want stays or walks away.

Life is about the "push, pull and carry". You experience pain so that you are pushed to find your true purpose. Hope then pulls you forward to fulfill your destiny. But to get to your destination, you must have faith that you are carried and supported by the Divine even if you don't see it. No matter what phase you are in, life is always working to get you where you are meant to be.

〉〉〉—————————————〈〈〈

The Universe is always trying to give you something of value. For every test or struggle, there is a miracle waiting to be accepted. Don't be so focused on what you think you want that you miss the real blessing. Be open to where life is trying to take you and accept the miracles you are given.

☀️DAY 207

Today stay patient and faithful. Believe God is holding your blessings until you are ready. Your experiences are preparing you to collect. Hearts must be opened to receive, and shoulders strengthened to carry abundance. Today make room for your delivery.

DAY 208

Many people pray for love and at the same time worry they will get hurt. This doubt closes your heart before you even open it. Why would your prayer be answered if you keep replacing your faith with fear? If you are having anxiety about maintaining love rather than finding love, you are not ready for it. You must believe that what you pray for will always get to you.

Life empowers you to have a breakthrough from a breakdown, so you can break an old habit. God is always pushing, pulling and carrying you. Pushing you to find your healing, pulling you to your purpose and carrying you to your destiny. Test and trials are necessary to reveal the best within you.

DAY 210

Everyone wishes for something, but not everyone receives. You can wish all you want, but you will never receive it if you don't put in the work. Wishing and working go hand in hand for the manifestation of miracles. You will never be paid in full if you don't put your full potential behind your dreams. Keep doing and going.

DAY 211

Today find your alignment by moving away from chasing what you think you want and allow life to reveal what you need. Chasing desires lead to temporary thrills that always expire. Go for the long-term play and align your experiences with the bigger vision for your life. When you flow with your purpose there is no expiration date or limit to the success life has for you.

Life can come at you full speed. Today respond by pushing above the mess so you can go harder. Friction is needed to have fruition. Pressure is necessary to generate pleasure. Chaos is needed to create order, and magic is essential for manifestation. Remember every seed must push through layers of soil and rock so it can bloom at its best. Keep going.

>>>———————————<<<

When you reach the point of manifesting your dreams, you will know it. This is when doubt creeps in and convinces you that you are on the edge of falling and failing. All edges have nothing to hold for security; which makes them scary. It is at this moment you must step out with faith and don't let doubt stop you from continuing your journey. You are not about to fall; you are about to fly.

☀️DAY 214

If you don't move past what hurts you, it will be difficult to move to what will heal you. Don't be ashamed to work on you; everyone has something they are trying to get over. Healing helps to bridge the gap between affliction so that you can create affection for yourself. Self-love and forgiveness are necessary for finding the fulfilment you seek. You will find your peace my friend.

How you show up for your life is how life shows up for you. Today push aside negative thoughts that cause you to act from fear or worry. If you fight life, it will send resistance your way. Believe that life is always working for you, ahead of you, and with you to give you what you need. Show up with positivity and receive your blessings. Flow don't fight.

DAY 216

Release yourself from the demand of how others think they should be loved. Your love will never be good enough. Many ask for love the way they think it should look, but that is not always the right way. People love how they are taught to love. How were you taught to love? You must own self-love to understand how to love others. Learn to give the love you own.

>>>———————————<<<

DAY 217

When you prayed today, you asked for love, abundance, peace plus more; and you probably already received your answer. Blessings never look like our prayers because God answers in seeds. Today, take another look and understand the power of the seed given. The blessing may be small, but with nurturing it will turn into something big.

>>> ———————————— <<<

DAY 218

Life will challenge you by continually pushing you toward what you are meant to do. If you resist, the struggle will persist. Let go of how you think your life should be and pay attention to where it is showing you to go. Stop forcing results and take comfort knowing what is meant for you will always get to you. Let go, align, and flow.

Today pray with faith and gratitude for the fruitful future that is already prepared for you. Invite success, cleared paths, healing, and unlimited abundance. Embrace the goodness in your life and work to create more of what you want. Say thank you for your daily provisions and manifested miracles as if they are guaranteed. Amen.

☀DAY 220

What you believe is what you create. No matter how difficult, focus on a new reality. Relax, regroup, let go, and allow your focus to narrow on hope. Believe that better is possible. Get excited about your present and your future. Keep your expectations positive by professing powerful words of prosperity and potential into your life. Transformation is continuously flowing to you.

You are not alone; everyone feels hopeless at some point. No matter how strong you have been in the past, there comes a time when you don't feel to fight. If you need the strength to move forward, look past your fight and focus on your progress. You have won at so many things in life, don't let one setback let you miss your set up for better. Keep going.

The hardest part of healing is accepting you are not. If your life is not where you want it to be, something is holding you back. Take a moment to look at the real you, not with criticism but with compassion. Allow yourself to embrace your wellbeing and welcome your healing positively. You have what it takes to overcome and triumph.

☀DAY 223

The hardest part of any struggle is staying hopeful and learning to think and feel differently. When you get overwhelmed, believing you are a winner seems impossible, but don't let the thought of creating change defeat you before you even start. Understand, the first step to the finish line will be your toughest and the most rewarding. Go for your happiness; you have what it takes to get it.

What's under the surface is more important than what you see above. If your prayers are delayed your signals to the Universe may be unclear. You cannot pray for love and don't feel self-love, pray for prosperity yet feel empty, pray for peace and feel attacked continuously. Get clear on what you want and don't let buried whispers overshadow your wishes. What you believe is what you become.

☀ DAY 225

Today give yourself patience, love, and compassion. You are doing the best you know with what you have learned. You create what you know. If what you know is not serving you, try embracing something new. You deserve what's right, not what's left after you serve others. Reconnect and give yourself the time you need to power and redirect your life.

DAY 226

We all have good days, challenging days and moments when we give up. Life is not always about perfection it's about persistence. Keep going, keep trying. You are doing the best you can, and some days that's what matters. Keep getting back in the fight even when you have been knocked down. No one is strong 100 percent of the time.

☀DAY 227

Gratitude is one of the most powerful emotions you can feel. It has a healing, magnifying power that can transform your hopefulness into happiness, joy into ecstasy, and peace into harmony. Find something good in your life, being thankful can amplify your ability to attract more abundance and wellbeing.

>>> ———————————— <<

Many of you are tired and exhausted from pushing through the dirt, fighting to get to your sunshine. You are ready to give up because you keep pushing with no way out. You might be going in the wrong direction. Push forward not backward. Leave what burdens you behind, release it, and lighten your load. You cannot advance with hands full of hurt. Let it all go.

Today acknowledge your gifts and use them to create the life you want. Embrace your unique talents and be proud because no one can do it like you. Crafting lifelong success takes patience and practice. The future you want takes time to build. Keep doing and going, what you work hard for will pay off soon.

Your blessings are all around you, look closer because they can appear in different stages of manifestation. You might be given a seed that needs to be planted, a shrub that requires nurturing to grow, or a tree that can be used for stability and shelter. Look at your life with hope and find what needs to be done to create your forest.

DAY 231

Experiences unfold to push you forward. The need to control how they should unfold is where disappointment can come in. Open yourself to what's promised by letting go of how you think your life ought to go. Trust your path because life wants you to win. You will repeatedly lose if you keep trying to manipulate the outcome. Let the fight go, and flow.

Life will turn you upside down for your cleansing. It will keep challenging you by resurfacing old wounds. Hurt will be repackaged and reproduced until it is resolved. If you don't face it and fix it, you will keep repeating it. Remove it by addressing it. You have what it takes to move forward by clearing your old and making room for new.

☀DAY 233

Change your focus today and find your peace. If you understand your purpose, you know you will be provided with what you need. Your pace is irrelevant. Let go of impatience and trust in Divine timing. Concentrate on your promise, be grateful for your provision, and have faith. What is meant for you will find you, don't block it with worry.

☀DAY 234

You don't have to rebuild a relationship with everyone you have forgiven. Forgiveness is not about forgetting; it is about moving forward from a past you wish was different. Forgive yourself and others. Make room in your heart to create better. The life you want requires focused positive energy. Don't delay building better by giving room in your heart to bitterness.

DAY 235

Don't let focusing on a little clutter distract you from seeing you are blessed. We all go through times of uncertainty and doubt. Know the mess is sent to distract you from your mission. Concentrate on your power of creation, not the chaos. You have what it takes to clear confusion while you create.

DAY 236

Be grateful today, not just for what you have, but what you have never gone through. Sometimes we get distracted by what we lack and never consider what we were saved from. Stay thankful, focused and keep pushing forward. You are more blessed than you know.

Set your eyes on things above you, not below you. Winning is about going up and onward. Focus forward on the positive. Don't let pain and trauma trump the hope in your heart. What you are looking for is also looking for you. Look with love and love will find you. Always reach up to receive.

# DAY 238

Change what you fight daily by focusing on your healing. Despair sets in when you highlight your sadness and lose sight of your confidence. You can move past the struggle by activating your hope and begin to flow. Look at your situation with the optimism of learning. Remember you don't lose you learn.

☀ DAY 239

Don't wait until you've reached your goal to be proud of yourself, be gratified by your journey. Joy is experienced in your wins along the way and should not be reserved for the destination. Today celebrate what you are doing to change your life. You have worked hard for every success you experience. Celebrate.

>>>———————————————⟨⟨⟨

If you are struggling, keep fighting. If you have been sacrificing, don't ever give up. If you feel defeated, remember help is always available. Where ever you are today, believe that it will get better. Keep going, keep showing up, and REFUSE to leave before your miracle happens.

Focus on your seeds not the blooms of others. Everyone is given their time to shine, never be discouraged. Don't get distracted from your promise because you are focused on temporary abundance. Be patient; your harvest will arrive at the right time. Blessings are often delayed because they are being prepared for permanency.

Asking then doubting with impatience will keep delaying your blessings. Focus on the promise, not the pace. If you genuinely believe in what you are destined for, then time is irrelevant. Stop rushing when things should happen and keep trusting in Divine timing. Years of abundance are better than moments of temporary thrills.

DAY 243

Be thankful for your struggles because without them you would not stumble across your strength. Every up, down, back and forth you have experienced is designed to bring out the real you. Every time you get knocked down teaches you how to find and develop your stance. Stand proudly in your power today.

We ask for success yet dislike the fame. We pray for abundance but don't want the responsibility. We ask for love yet get tired giving it. Remember every position has its pain. The best fruits have bitter outsides and sweet insides. Learn to appreciate the entire fruit, because nothing is ever 100% perfect. Whatever is your bitter, enjoy it because it comes with a lot of sweet.

Blessings and miracles cannot be poured into your life if you have no opening to receive them. Many of you pray for abundance yet make no room in your heart and life to receive them. There must be an opening for success to be poured. Today create a big space to receive the abundant goodness you work hard for. Believe it is yours to receive.

Sometimes the burdens you carry are significant because they are designed to strengthen you for big blessings. You will always be sent a challenge that reveals the warrior within you. Triumph by not getting distracted with the battle, but by focusing on the victory. When you concentrate on the promise, you understand the fight always has a purpose.

>>>————————————————————«««

DAY 247

Making that first step to create happiness can be hard, but necessary. Don't let fear freeze you from moving forward. Just start, stay present, and take it one day at a time, one step at a time. Focus on how you are able, not how you are disabled. Remember it is a series of continual steps, no matter how strong or shaky, that make up a fulfilling journey.

Everyone chases what they think is lacking in their lives. You are taught to look on the outside for what you have not discovered on the inside. Stop looking for love and happiness, because it is already within fighting to come out. You are amazing. Take the time today to go within and discover your greatness.

Impatience is a form of doubt. When you rush to get results life will keep giving you resistance. If you truly understand that what is yours will come to you in the right moment, you will release the focus on time. Remain patient and trust in Divine timing. When you think you are down to nothing, the Universe is up to something. Stay patient and trust.

DAY 250

You experience disappointment when you let your attachment to outcomes control what you believe should happen in your life. What is meant for you will never miss you and what is sent to you is intended to teach and create a new you. Let go of what you think you should have gained and look at what you have achieved. Don't let disappointment keep distracting you from your destiny.

How do you talk to yourself when no one is listening? Are your words kind, patient, compassionate and accepting? If this is not how you talk, you are doing yourself a disservice. Everyone needs encouraging, loving and uplifting words and the loudest, most important voice is your own. You are the closest to your ear, pay attention to what you whisper. It will manifest in your life.

>>>———————————<<<

COMMANDING LIFE

Finding your purpose begins with looking at the one thing that is unique to you. You overlook it because it is the most natural thing for you to create. Every up, down, yes, and no has taught you something, focus on the message as it is the secret to your fulfilment. The lesson that is taking you the longest to learn unlocks your purpose.

☀DAY 253

When life says 'hold' do just that. Trust that your delay does not mean denied. Don't get anxious get quiet and listen for what needs to be done before you get the 'go'. Sometimes you are delayed because the area you have prepared for your blessings is not big enough. Don't let 'hold' make you feel helpless, get hopeful for a bigger harvest.

Thank you for healing my heart and guiding me forward. Thank you for revealing my path and showing me how to accept my purpose. Thank you for the ability and opportunity to create prosperity in my life. Thank you for directing me to the peace I seek. Today, I am grounded in gratitude and welcome Divine miracles manifesting. Amen

☀️DAY 255

If you see yourself as a person on a mission, what you pray for will change. You will understand that what you need most to succeed is commitment and the ability to overcome the obstacles in your way. Learn to master your path and you will achieve your purpose. Remember, prayer is needed for the journey, not the destination.

DAY 256

When there is a purpose for your day nothing can hold you back from accomplishing your mission. You begin to praise your life for the ups and downs because it all has a part to play. Don't give up when it does not look like your dreams. Instead express gratitude for the valleys and the mountaintops. Before you earn the right to be thankful up top, you must be thankful down below.

Today's prayer, "I am committed to becoming who I need to be to live the highest vision for my life. I have all that I need and want as life flows to me and I flow with it. As I work on my purpose, I am Divinely guided, supported, protected and loved. Thank you, Universe, for always steering me toward the best life has to offer me. Amen."

☀️DAY 258

Procrastination and perfection are partners to insecurity. Both hold you back from realizing your full potential. To overcome, you must focus on the higher vision for your life and stop living the version that is not fulfilling you. When you have a clear vision, and a focused 'why,' you will never have to convince yourself to work for what you want to keep.

You can't get over anything until you give up what you thought it should have been. Many get lost in the illusion of the past rather than the reality of it. Remember, what's meant for you will never leave you, don't get stuck wishing it should have stayed. Sometimes your temporary dreams must shatter to reveal the REAL dreams you forgot.

The answer is "yes!" Your dreams will come true. Keep believing in yourself and your prayers. The actions you are taking, the inner work you are doing, all will pay off soon. You have what it takes, just keep going. Don't doubt, DO. Time loses its power when you have a purpose. Trust in Divine timing.

>>> ———————— <<<

DAY 261

Find your best self by focusing on the good in your life. When you ground yourself with gratitude, greatness will manifest daily. Commit to working on your healing and finding your joy and balance. When you operate from your happy self, life becomes easier. Success starts with you. Your love is lovely; today recognize that.

DAY 262

Believe you will get what you work for. When uncertainty sets in, focus on what you need to create to thrive. Trust in the unlimited possibilities despite the current 'no.' What is ordered for your life will always manifest despite time and circumstances. Stay faith FULL that your promise will be delivered.

# DAY 263

Today's message is simple. You are what you expect. Expect the best always. Sending the best your way, it is up to you to decide how it is received.

When you are down to nothing, the Universe is up to something. If you don't currently see a miracle, be patient, your magic will manifest. Your setback is setting you up for the biggest comeback of your life. Remember you are always supported. Believe change is happening, even if you do not see it.

Can you afford the delay? You want to see change and greatness manifest in your life, but fear freezes you from moving forward. Every moment you stay stuck in fear delays all that you want to achieve. You are a powerful creator with the ability to transform your life. Don't let the illusion of the impossible keep you from your possible.

Always believe that nothing is going wrong. When you think that things are falling apart, understand it is only falling into place. Sometimes foundations need to break for you to rebuild and become. Life will upgrade and transform you for your promise. Remember the harder the path, the higher the levels attained.

To live your best life, you must be your best self. Being your best self is not about resisting but embracing your power with reaction. Yes, life happens, but how you respond to the setback creates the setup. Life will always send obstacles; only you can control what is yielded after. You can retreat and stay small or push forward and create big.

DAY 268

Many fail because they try to be disciplined before they become committed. Commitment is the state of being dedicated. Discipline is the practice of said dedication. Before you can make any change in your life, commit to YOU. Once you commit to your happiness, you develop the discipline to deal with ALL. Commit, then the change you desire will come.

>>>———————————<<<

DAY 269

You must know pain to know love. Struggle to recognize success. Be at the bottom to understand the importance of the rise to the top. Be thankful for it all and rise. Use hope and faith to strengthen you for the journey. Hope that nothing remains the same, and faith that you are destined for the best. Climb my friend, climb.

>>> ———————————— <<<

You deserve the best and should have the best life has to offer. But are you at your best to receive it? When you become your best self, you attract the best for you. What is highest for you is always waiting for you to claim it. Instead of wishing for it, put effort into being it. The best of life will then flow to you naturally.

Yes, it is hard to make a change. Yes, it is hard to move forward. Yes, it is hard to let go. But not working for your happiness is even harder. Every moment you procrastinate because you think working on it is hard, is time wasted in fear, not faith. Faith does not work unless you work. Only you can put effort into your happiness.

☀️DAY 272

Empower yourself through action. Push doubt away and find what you can do to get where you need to go. You have what it takes to create the life you want, it all starts with believing. You are destined for a life you cannot presently perceive because you aren't looking high enough. Don't let the clouds block you from understanding that sunshine exists.

☀️DAY 273

Sitting back and wishing for your life to improve, will not make it better unless you work. Life meets you where you meet it. If you always say, "it is hard," life will keep giving you challenges. Everyone has trials, but the power is in your reaction. Take back your control by putting it into the creation of a new life. You must work for your life to work.

>>> ———————————— <<<

DAY 274

Are you open to being better than you can imagine? Take a second to consider what you see for yourself, because it may be limited from your point of view. Sometimes you cannot see the mountaintop because you are focused on the valley. If what you see now is keeping you doubtful, don't believe it, it is your time to rise. Believe the top exists, and start climbing, my friend.

☀DAY 275

"Thank you" is the word; gratitude is the feeling. Praying with gratitude for a positive outcome is the fastest way to manifest what you seek. You must know, feel, do, then receive. If you are praying and asking, make a change to praying and thanking. Profess thankfulness, feel gratefulness, and act daily. Only then you will see a difference.

>>>———————————————<<<

DAY 276

Everyone wants to move forward. No one wants to keep saying they want better. You are the lead in your life, and that means the decision to move forward is yours. Yes, moving on and letting go is hard, but staying stuck and never realizing happiness is harder. The choice to be better and have better is yours. Exercise your right to decide today.

☀DAY 277

Express gratitude today for your deliverance and success. Pray with confidence that it is on its way to you. Move past 'asking' for what you want and start 'thanking' for it. If you expect a positive outcome, then you believe it will happen for you. Put power into your words and actions. Create the change you want in your life.

>>>———————————————<<<

You are what you expect. Are you expecting love, success, healing, peace and manifested miracles? The most powerful words you can speak starts with "I am." Let your affirmation statement today be what you expect in your life tomorrow. Say it, believe it, then go out and create it. Expect the best, always.

☀DAY 279

You are already winning. Everything you asked for is around you. You prayed for prosperity and you were given skills to create it. You asked for love; it is within you ready to be shared. You asked for peace, sit still and embrace it. What you seek exists in your life right now. Acknowledge its presence, profess your gratitude, and embrace your power to create more.

COMMANDING LIFE

Unworthiness is a lie you tell yourself when you don't feel you are destined for greatness. Every single person has a promise; you must believe in it and go for it. You deserve all the happiness life has to offer. Make the decision today to become your promise. Claim it and then create it. Your life will not work unless you work.

When a door closes, express your gratitude. It does not mean you are denied; it is a signal to look again. Don't get so focused on a closed door that you miss YOUR opened door. It is ready and waiting for you to enter. Stop, look up and embrace where you are supposed to be. Sometimes life gives you what you need, not what you want.

Today reconnect, refocus and recommit. Reconnect with the good in you, refocus on finding the better you, and recommit to creating the best you. The answers you seek have already been delivered. Remember you are given seeds, plant them and be fruitful. Give them time to grow as everything has a season.

 DAY 283

Don't confuse what you are offered with what you are worth. Many people provide love from their level of understanding, and that should never be your interpretation of love. Don't let your experiences with past love overshadow what is true. Real love is out there. The only way you will know how to distinguish it is by having it with yourself.

>>> ———————————— <<<

Today's prayer: I am thankful for the infinite opportunities, abundance, peace, healing and opening doors in my life. Blessings and prosperity flow easily to me, and I am Divinely guided to my happiness. My paths are cleared, and miracles materialize. I am thankful for the transforming mindset that allows me to steadfastly pursue the life that I want. Amen.

>>> ———————————————— <<<

☀DAY 285

Pursuing happiness after disappointment requires bravery, commitment, and action. Believe that life will get better by developing the discipline to act and go after the best. You have what it takes to pursue the life you want. Remember, mistakes are only missed steps. Regroup, refocus, realign your efforts and always keep stepping forward.

>>>———————————<<<

DAY 286

Reality check, no one is coming to save you. No money, job or relationship can bring you happiness. Only you can do this. If life throws a rock at you, catch it and build a house of security. If it throws dirt at you, plant a seed that will become a forest of prosperity. Use what you have and create the life YOU want. Understand "self-first" is not selfish, your happiness will materialize, and nothing can ever change that.

>>>———————————<<<

Don't resist when life needs to cleanse the old and welcome the new. The pain people experience is not in the letting go but in the resisting of the flow. What you need will never be forced and is always coming to you. Stop holding on to what needs to be purged, focus on freeing your hands to receive. You will never have to fight to keep what is meant for you.

>>>———————————<<<

Today make a change in how you create because lives can be built on fear or faith. Consider this, if you have had any success driven by fear, try to imagine what you will manifest if you power your life with faith. They say faith can move mountains, put your faith to the test today. Go out and move the mountain blocking your way. You've got this!

☀️ DAY 289

Ignored stuff turns into a big pile of ignored stuff. It won't go away unless you clear it up. You can't keep resisting and retreating from clearing your clutter. Ignored pain will keep resurfacing and shaking your life up unless it is healed. Face it, learn from it, deal with it and most importantly use it. Don't fear it, create from it, because amazing things grow from dirt.

>>> ———————————— <<<

Falling and failing are natural parts of the cycle of life. Mishaps will show up to teach and take you to your next levels. It is in these stumbles you understand one of the biggest lessons in life: "You are the creator of what happens after the struggle." When you fall or fail, only you can create your success or your stuck. What will you create today for your tomorrow?

DAY 291

As seasons and reasons change, the old gets cleansed and new gets formed. Life is always purging, producing and pushing you toward your highest self. Everyone has a purpose and fighting its pursuit can cause struggle. Sometimes what you see for yourself is limited because you don't look high enough. Stop resisting your path and flow to your unlimited possibilities.

DAY 292

Letting go of what you think you want is hard, but if it causes pain, then it is not what you need. Don't hold on because you don't want to lose out on a dream. Ask yourself if this is the last dream you will ever have, or can you create new dreams? Trust that letting go is cleansing an illusion or breaking and rebuilding a new foundation. Stay faithful and patient; the purpose is always revealed.

COMMANDING LIFE

You cannot love someone into loving you right. Many people love today expecting to be seen and appreciated tomorrow. Hoping to eventually be loved the right way only brings disappointment in the now. Real love sees, values and appreciates, always. Today, understand your worth and stop discounting it for a future payoff.

When life brings resistance, the real fight is not losing sight of who you are and remembering your capabilities. Who you are and who you are meant to be can get lost in the battle to survive. Don't let struggle keep you stuck. Today, stop trying to find your way, instead create a way. No matter what you face, remember you write your chapters. You have what it takes to push through with a new self-creation story.

>>>———————<<<

Many get distracted with the need for immediate resolution and spend little time meditating or going within to receive a guided answer. Today take the time to listen to your heart and head before you act. Move past reacting with only emotion and add mindfulness so you can flow. Peace will only be found when your heart and head align for the solutions you seek.

>>> ———————————— <<<

DAY 296

You cannot be heard if you don't speak. You cannot reap if you don't sow. You cannot heal if you don't face and fix your hurt. You cannot find peace if you don't get quiet. Whatever you are searching for in life, it is one action away. Speak, sow, fix and get quiet because life wants you to have what you lack. It won't get better unless you actively create better.

Yes, you are tired, but just beyond that weariness is your awakening. There is a difference between giving up and taking a rest. Today, take a minute to regroup, recharge, reset and find what will empower you to push forward. Everyone needs time to rest and refuel before they keep going. You have what it takes to advance; sometimes you must go through neutral before you move into drive.

>>>———————————<<<

COMMANDING LIFE

DAY 298

Work on you, not your
destination. Life never changes
your blessings; it only keeps
pushing you to get prepared to
receive them. Your miracles are
already arranged, have faith in
that guarantee. Today do the
work and get ready for where
you are going; it will be worth
it. You must be whole and
healed, to handle the
happiness coming your way.

>>> ————————————— <<<

☀DAY 299

Find yourself, and you will always find your way. Let the greatness in you radiate despite what you face. Don't ever doubt your ability to accomplish your dreams. Rejoice in the blessings and Divine miracles coming your way. Purpose attracts possibilities, and gratitude attracts greatness. Today is your day!

>>>———————————<<

# DAY 300

Fights are necessary to reveal the warrior within and strengthen your focus. The art of war says to concentrate on the plan for victory and do not get distracted by the difficulty of battle. When you focus on your promise, you understand the fight has a purpose. Choose strategy over struggle and welcome success.

DAY 301

The need to have control with perfection is a symptom of self-doubt. This uncertainty generates worry and blocks your ability to create solutions. Find peace by understanding nothing will ever be 100% perfect. Accept, acknowledge, and let go of the concept of control. Every position has its pain, and every step and stumble have a purpose. Believe in your abilities and go for it.

DAY 302

Making that first step toward creating your happiness can be hard, but it is necessary. Don't let doubt keep delaying you from moving forward. Just start, stay present, take it slow, yet steady. Concentrate on how you are able not how you are disabled. Be consistent at being consistent and commit to your happiness. Where you are going will be worth it.

Sometimes your investments are tested with time to reveal their permanency. You cannot expect to act today and receive today. You cannot expect to pray today and get a resolution today. How much time and effort you put into your dreams is always rewarded. Patience is essential to a purpose; you have a lifetime to reap the rewards.

DAY 304

Today focus on the unlimited potential and possibilities around you. Be grateful for the abundance of goodness in the simple things. Open yourself to a new attitude of gratitude, prosperity, and joy. Trust that all is well and move forward with a renewed sense of assurance and hope. Don't worry, only welcome. What is for you will never miss you, put faith in that.

Setups and setbacks are continuous because they are the cycle of life. Learning to embrace the constant change is the lesson that we all take the longest to learn. Have faith in the process because every up, down, back and forth has a purpose. Believe nothing is going wrong so you can learn and get to the right faster. You've got this.

You can reap what you sow, therefore setting the right intention for your life is important. When you make your decisions, create from a place of love not hurt. Choices made from hurt can create a massive mess. Remember hurt people hurt people. Before you act, set the right intentions and create from positivity. Miracles will manifest in a life built on purpose.

DAY 307

Impatience is a form of fear and doubt. When you keep rushing to get results life will keep giving you resistance. If you truly understand that what is yours will come to you in the right season, you will release your focus on the clock. Remain patient and trust in Divine timing. When you think you are down to nothing, the Universe is up to something. Stay patient and faith FULL.

>>> ———————— <<<

You experience disappointment when you let what you want overshadow what you need. Life is always working to give you what you need. What is meant for you will never miss you, and what is sent to you is intended to teach and create a new you. Let go of what you think you should have gained and look at what you did achieve.

If you prayed for hurt to go away, practice self-healing. If you prayed for abundance, practice planting before harvesting. If you prayed for love, practice self-love. Whatever you pray for must be worked on before it can exist in your life. Be patient, prepare, practice and persist. Prayers are answered on the journey, not at the destination.

Time cannot be saved for future use, but it can be invested in the future you. What you do today creates your tomorrow. You cannot wish for what you want; you must work for it. Planted seeds are not immediately fruitful and take time, nurturing, and effort to manifest. You have what it takes, don't let impatience keep you from planting.

DAY 311

Many people believe that when you get what you pray for you will be happy. Remember, when prayers are answered, you then get more to pray for. Life will always keep you praying despite the abundance of blessings. Stop praying for problems to go away and start thanking for the ability to overcome what comes your way. There will always be a need for prayer.

>>>———————————————————<<<

DAY 312

The change in season is designed to test your resilience. Always creating and reevaluating your dreams is what life is about. Every season has a reason for your progress. Changes and challenges are what you need to learn to walk until it works. Life is like a seed without instructions; you must keep planting and nurturing until it finally blooms.

DAY 313

Stop trying to fix other people's problems. Focus on fixing your own. Allow life to bless you by focusing on your healing. Many pray for deliverance from hurt but cannot see it already exists because they are distracted by another's healing. Their healing will not improve your life or change your past. Only your healing will bring the happiness you seek. Get consistent at making change happen in your life.

DAY 314

If you are steadfast at your work, your wishes will manifest. Don't quit because answers aren't coming as quickly as you want. Despite the storms, do not abandon ship, take control and ride it out. Blessings always manifest right after the moment you want to quit. Life is only testing your resilience.

DAY 315

When you have been through a season of struggle and stillness, believe the next natural step to experience is movement. Have faith that what you experience today, will change tomorrow if you do the work. Keep moving, climbing, trusting and welcoming your blessings. Don't give up before the miracle manifests. Keep going.

# DAY 316

Don't forfeit your blessings because you are afraid to manage your setbacks. When life sends a challenge don't get stuck, push forward and take control with your responses. Look at your past achievements for assurance that you have what it takes to step over the struggle and step into success. Believe you are worthy and welcome the prosperity and peace you pray for.

>>>———————————<<<

See yourself on a mission of guaranteed success and change what you pray for. Understand that what you need most to ensure the win is commitment and the ability to overcome the obstacles in your way. Once you master your mental might, you push through anything. Remember, prayer is needed for the journey, not the destination.

DAY 318

You are only moved into your position of promise when you are ready. Everything you have gone through helps with the principles you need to prosper. You must be able to manage the down before the up, the little before the plenty, and the rejection before the affection. Remember, nothing is going wrong. Stay faith FULL; your prosperity is already prepared.

DAY 319

When you put purpose into your day, nothing can hold you back from accomplishing your goals. You begin to understand the reasons for the seasons and refuse to give up on your dreams. Today refocus and express gratitude for your valleys and mountaintops. Before you can earn the right to be thankful up top, you must be thankful down below.

>>>———————————<<<

Change is feared when you don't trust your abilities. Believe you can create the happiness you want. Success begins when you understand you are equipped with what you need. Do you think you went through all that struggle and strengthening for nothing? Don't be distracted by what you did not get, focus on the skills you learned and commit to crushing your goals. You've got this.

Never let doubt win. Combat the feeling by repeating the affirmation: "I choose faith over fear." Repeat it as many times as you need to and conquer the doubt with DO. DO believe you are worthy. DO believe you have the power to overcome. Most of all, DO believe you can create the life you want. Your life will transform when you change your doubt into DO.

Stop complaining about what you go through and start 'thanking' for them. Thank every closed door, because they directed you to your opened door. Being good does not always mean you get good, but you will learn what is good for you. Push forward and be a victor. Experiences are meant to have you question the progress of your life and push you to your promise.

Creation requires commitment and won't manifest without work. Yes, taking the first step to making the life you want comes with a little discomfort, but nothing will happen unless you go for it. Don't stay small because you doubt your abilities. Go big, brave and bold and show the world your capabilities. If you don't bet on yourself, no one else will. Go for it; you can do it!

>>> ———————— <<<

Learn to appreciate your lessons, not resist them. Everything you survived has prepared you for your purpose and is valuable to your happiness. Trials and triumph teach you what is important and who is important. How else would you know who has your back? You may lose people along the way, but never your purpose. Trust in your path.

☀DAY 325

Find a reason to course correct rather than complain. You have plenty to be thankful for, take the time to look. One of your biggest blessings is the opportunity to make a change. Life will reward you with twice as much because you worked the bitter and created your better. Remember, gratitude grounds and allows you to grow into your greatness.

>>>———————————<<<

The happiness you have been working on is coming. Everyone has the faith to do and go, but many do not have the confidence to wait. Just when it's about to happen you begin to question your "Yes." Let go of the doubt and keep doing; you already got your answer. Stop worrying about the when, start welcoming the win.

☀DAY 327

Move past being stuck in self-pity and find success in self-compassion. Today face what you need to heal and get whole. Don't get so distracted helping others that you forget your self-servicing. Don't ignore your 'check engine' alert any longer. Take the time to fuel your faith by focusing on you first. When you are running at your best, you deliver your greatest performances.

Get clear on what you welcome into your life. Many want happiness and have no clue what that looks like for them. Then to add to the mess, they pressure the Universe to make 'it' happen. You must get clear on what you want before it can be delivered. The lack of clarity will delay your delivery. Your intentions are the invitation to miracles, start setting them.

>>>———————————<<<

☀DAY 329

Don't let your doubt keep you from the destination. Stop looking back fearing falling or looking forward dreading how far you must travel. Focus on what you need to do at this moment to keep your pace progressing. Slow and steady is better than hurried and unsure. Your climb is not worried about your pace, you are. Be here now.

>>>———————————————<<<

"Nothing is going wrong," tell yourself that 1,000 times a day if you need to. Every twist, turn, up and down is necessary for your betterment and is part of a plan to give you what you need to fulfill your purpose. You must trust in it all because you are not where you need to be by chance. The faster you learn to see the purpose of ALL, the more efficiently you create the OUT.

People are afraid to climb, not because they fear the mountain, but because they do not trust they have what it takes to succeed. Everyone is given what they need to live a life of happiness. Trust that you can find joy by using what you already have. Yes, you have stumbled, but you were always supported, and never fell off. Take a second today and celebrate your progress.

The answers to your prayers are always given in seeds. Plant them, be faithful and stay patient as they grow. Let go of the need to rush the process by projecting your doubt with 'when' and 'how.' Time is your test for the worthiness of the reward. Your magic will materialize when you spend the time invested in the work, not watching the clock.

There are things in life that come easy, and there are others that require you to work. Don't get distracted by the fatigue of working and ignore what you already have. There is happiness around you, appreciate it no matter the form of delivery. Being grateful for your existing blessings will welcome more miracles manifesting.

DAY 334

Life is always directing you to where you need to go to accomplish your purpose. The journey becomes a struggle when you push against the pulls, and fight with the flow. Let go of the control you think you need to win and welcome the guidance. Remember you are always Divinely supported, protected and loved.

☼DAY 335

Life changes when you focus on what you gained, not what you lack. It is human nature to see what is missing rather than what was manifested. You are not where you are by chance. Life wants you to win; therefore it pours blessings slowly to teach you how to prepare for the plenty. You must learn to manage what you have before you can manage what you pray for.

>>>———————————————————————————————————————⟨⟨⟨

DAY 336

With grace and gratitude, allow life to remove what does not serve your happiness. Remember clearing and creation require time. Today, welcome what makes you whole and helps you heal. Stay patient throughout the transitions. Remember you never lose, you only learn who you are. That makes you a winner.

Resilience, rejection, receiving and redemption are all parts of the cycle of life. Seasons have reasons, and it is all necessary to your journey. You are always blessed; it is with gratitude you recognize this. Whatever stage you are in, know you have what it takes to get through it and to get to the win. Keep going.

Stop trying to create a new life with old thinking and habits. Every stage of your life will require a new you and a new way of thinking. Education has its levels, and so does life. You must learn better, to do better. Elementary thinking won't get you the mastered life you seek.

☀DAY 339

Do you truly understand how blessed you are? Sometimes you get distracted looking at what others have that you miss what you gained. Everyone has a specific path with different arrival times. Don't get distracted by someone's temporary blessing and miss the permanent blessing that is trying to come into your life. Welcome your win.

# DAY 340

Today find peace in the beauty that is your life. Many get focused on what they think is not manifesting and don't see the miracle that is already unfolding. You have been looking for peace, love, and happiness, yet miss that the existing shakeup is cleansing what's not serving you. Stop resisting, let go and welcome ALL that you need to thrive.

>>> ———————— <<<

☀DAY 341

The Universe is sending you healing as we speak. What you think you lack is a lesson in planting and patience. You must know how to live without, to understand living with. How else will you appreciate the abundance and the beauty of your harvest? Lack is a lesson on learning the importance of living with gratitude.

Do not choose misery over miracles because you are not willing to put in the work. Many are stuck in places they do not want to be because they refuse to push themselves to higher. Your miracle is one action away, don't let struggle keep you from making that key step to your success. Don't wish for it, work for it.

Today pray for the grace and dignity to release what you do not need. Ask for the ability to clean and clear without creating another mess. Allow what needs to be eliminated to be put aside with poise. Make room for your plenty by welcoming unlimited prosperity and possibilities.

Recognize that you have been supported, shielded, guided and loved. Supported with what you need to get to your healing. Shielded from struggles you could not survive. Guided to what you needed to thrive and loved deeply because you have been winning. Today, take a moment to celebrate your progress and Divine protection.

☀DAY 345

You cannot give from nothing; therefore, you must understand "self-first" is not selfish. Fueling you first is important for all. Self-first is giving you what you need on the inside to manage what shows up on the outside. Once you are at your best, you will provide yourself with the best, your best to others, and the best to your life. Creating greatness starts within and shows up without.

# DAY 346

Everywhere you have been prepared you for where you are going. You are born with a purpose, and it is your choice to pursue it. Find yourself, and you will understand your real power. Every chapter of your life is teaching you your capacity to carry and create. There are no mistakes along the way.

You are not being blocked; you are being made. Have faith, even with Divine power; the earth took time to create. You are built from every brick thrown at you, and every seed you have ever planted. Be patient with the process because it is clearing the temporary to manifest the permanent. A strong foundation is not built by chance.

Only you can create the quality of your life through your choices. It is human nature to focus on the trying and discard the triumphs. Life isn't about what struggle you go through, what love you lost, or what you lack. Life is about how you respond to ALL. Triumph over your experiences by taking back your power and exercising your choice to create.

☀️DAY 349

Hope is one of the most powerful feelings you can have because it gives you an expectation of better when you taste bitter. Have faith in your prayers and keep working for what you want. Today celebrate all that you have created to live a life of happiness. Your joy is in the journey that you are on now. Celebrate your progress.

>>>———————————————————<<<

Take a moment today to reflect on the life you are blessed with. Sometimes we get distracted by the lack and miss the love we have surrounding us. Life has prevented you from circumstances you cannot even imagine. Praised the closed doors and the numerous 'no,' because they were your protection. How amazing is that?

Don't forget your worth. Whatever you do in life remember your service is valuable. Don't let the fear of losing affection, recognition or appreciation keep you from expressing your magic. Do not discount your time, love, abilities or talents because of others. See your value always.

DAY 352

Going within is a form of self-love. Many fear the stillness because they dread what they will see. You cannot fix what you don't face, and you cannot course correct if you don't know how to direct the driver. Get still and connect with who is steering your life. You won't see change without unless you create change from within.

☀DAY 353

Your journey is yours. What levels you climb, what success you achieve, is unique to you. Where others are in their journey should never distract you, focus on your steps. Don't let the perception of where you need to be, dictate the pace of your progress. Personal growth is a manifestation of your walk, not theirs. Travel your road as you see fit.

>>>————————————<<<

DAY 354

Create your life from three principles: vision, intent, and action. Vision because you must know where you are going before you go. Intention because you must be clear on why you want your happiness. Act because you must work for it instead of wish for it. Get clear on all these, and you will create the life you want.

DAY 355

When you think you are about to break, life will show you just how well you are built. Free yourself from your burdens by letting go of the mountain you carry, because you were only meant to climb it. Move past the control of holding on, and believe you were designed to succeed. Just think, if you can carry a mountain, imagine your capacity to carry abundant blessings.

DAY 356

Remember, before you are fully blessed you may still be challenged. Right when you are about to have a breakthrough, your faith will be tested again. Don't let the last few questions in the exam distract you from your progress. They are sent there to verify your commitment to your victory. Don't quit now, keep going.

☀DAY 357

Today stop, look and love. Stop and feel gratitude for what you have overcome to achieve your happiness. Look and observe how beautifully your progress is unfolding. Love and accept who you are becoming. The beauty is in the journey not in the destination. Appreciate every step forward and welcome more success to celebrate.

>>>———————————<<<

Are you spinning your wheels or working on your happiness? Know the difference between keeping yourself distracted with 'busy work' and being productive. Progress is made when you do the work to get what you wish for. Don't hope for the miracle and leave the work to the Universe. Remember life meets you where you meet it.

☀DAY 359

Do not underestimate the power you can produce from the pain you have passed. Friction and focus create fire! Light the fire within by finding who you are, and you will find your purpose. Stop waiting for the light at the end of the tunnel. Light your way through using the fire within.

☀DAY 360

Many are focused on future happiness not understanding that the only way to be truly fulfilled is to embrace this moment. The joy you wish for is unfolding in the present. It is in the smiles of the ones you love; the laughs you share with friends and the moments you celebrate your success. The next time your mind wanders into the future, refocus on your now.

DAY 361

The real struggle for happiness begins on the inside and is reflected on the life you create on the outside. Hearts must be healed and whole to welcome lasting fulfillment and joy. If life is not what you imagine, you have the power to change it. Work on how you thrive on the inside, and it will blossom on the outside.

>>> ———————— <<<

☀️ DAY 362

Sometimes you must look back and be grateful for what you were saved from, rather than look at what you did not gain. You have been protected from things you cannot imagine. Don't forget to recognize that was a blessing. Today be grateful for being supported, guided and loved by forces unseen. Call it God, Universe or whatever you like, acknowledge the Divine has your back.

COMMANDING LIFE

☀DAY 363

Sometimes we take less than because we do not see our worth. We go above and beyond because we fear losing affection. Today take a step back and honestly look at the value you bring. You are beautiful, strong, remarkable and loving. Believe in your abilities, they have gotten you this far and will take you to unimaginable places.

>>>———————<<<

You have gotten your 'yes,' let go of the when and how your victory will happen. Release your dependency on time and understand nothing is going wrong. Don't let doubt make you block the beauty of the unfolding. What is for you always shows up when you are ready. Be amazed by the miracle, not the momentum.

DAY 365

Today's prayer: I welcome support, healing and wholeness. Support to create positive actions that serve the betterment of my life. Healing to understand self-love, sharing love, being loved and welcoming love. Wholeness that helps me live with faith not fear. I welcome my miracles manifesting daily. Amen.

>>>————————————<<<

COMMANDING LIFE

☀️DAY 366

COMMANDING LIFE

Join our online communities:

 CommandingLife.com

@CommandingLife   @Commanding_Life

Thank You